UNITT'S
CLOCK PRICE GUIDE

BY
PETER UNITT AND ANNE WORRALL

Fitzhenry & Whiteside

AN ORIGINAL CANADIAN PUBLICATION

© 1991 - Fitzhenry & Whiteside
No part of this book may be reproduced in any
form without permission in writing from the
publisher: Fitzhenry & Whiteside
195 Allstate Parkway
Markham, Ontario
L3R 4T8

Canadian Cataloguing in Publication Data
Unitt, Peter, 1914-
  Unitt's clock price guide

Includes bibliographical references and index.
ISBN 1-55041-057-1

1. Clocks and watches - Prices. 2. Clocks and
watches - Collectors and collecting. 3. Clocks
and watches - Europe. 4. Clocks and watches -
North America. I. Unitt, Joan, 1915.
II. Worrall, Anne. III. Title.

NK7499.U55 1991   681.1'13'075   C91-093374-X

Printed and Bound in Canada
by John Deyell Company

INTRODUCTION

An enthusiastic collector once remarked that if God had wanted us to have the perfect collectable he would have invented the clock. It is said that clocks were first used in monasteries to call the monks to prayer, so maybe He did give one of the monks a nudge. The rest is history and many a happy soul out there has found that the purchase or gift of a clock has lead to a lifelong urge to adopt and nurture them in ever increasing numbers.

Old clocks are popular everywhere and this has lead to scarcity, but do not despair there are little nuggets out there waiting to be mined. Prices have risen along with those of all good things, but the enthusiast will always find treasures.

The values in this guide are taken from many sources, but it should be borne in mind that there is no perfect guide, someone will always pay more and another will get the same item for less. The prices represent values for clocks in good working order.

We wish to express our gratitude to all those who have been kind enough to help us. It is not possible to mention everyone by name, however, we would like to offer special thanks to the following: Peter Griffiths, Irene and George Hartwick, Paul Kingston, Bob McDonald, Lois and Bob Miller, Frank Thornton, and Frank Williams.

Good hunting, may you find the treasures you seek.

CONTENTS

CANADIAN CLOCKS

Above — Left —
CANADA CLOCK CO.
"Victoria" with drawer. 8-day
mirror mantel clock, hour strike.
Primary wood walnut, gilded
figures at sides, original glass.
Ca. 1872. Ht. 24" . . $1200.00

Above — Right —
CANADA CLOCK CO.
"Victoria" Second style, no
drawer. 8-day, hour and ½-hour
strike. Flying horse finials not
original. Ht. 22½" . .   850.00

Left —
CANADA CLOCK CO.
"Tilley." 30-hour mantel clock,
hour strike. Carved walnut case,
all original including frosted
glass and pendulum. Ca. 1872.
Ht. 19" 800.00

CANADA CLOCK CO. "Niagara."
8-day mantel clock, hour strike.
Walnut case, all original including
frosted glass. Ca. 1872.
Ht. 23" $1000.00

CANADA CLOCK CO.
"City of Paris" 30-hour, time
and hour strike. All original.
Ht. 19" $950.00

Canada Clock Co.
Whitby, Ontario
1872 - 1875

Canada Clock Co.
Hamilton, Ontario
1880 - 1884

Left —
CANADA CLOCK CO. 8-day
regulator, time only. Walnut case.
Ca. 1872. Ht. 22" $1200.00

6

CANADA CLOCK CO. OGEE. 30-hour strike with weights. Mahogany veneer on pine, mirror door. Ht. 26" $325.00

NEWHAVEN 30-HOUR OGEE. Made for James Grant, Stouffville, Ontario. Ca. 1865. . . . . $225.00

CANADIAN OGEE WOOD CLOCK. 30-hour wood movement. Made by R.B. Field & Co. Brockville, Canada. $300.00

CANADIAN COLUMN CLOCK.
Made by Horace Burr, Dundas,
Upper Canada.
Ca. 1860 . . . .$1600.00

PILLAR CLOCK.
30-hour. "Extra No. 1 brass
clock made expressly for
B.B. Bartlett, Canada West
by Seth Thomas."
Ca. 1860.
Ht. 25" $325.00

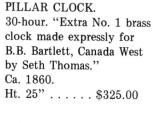

UPPER CANADA CLOCK. Movement by Riley Whiting.
Elaborately carved case by H. Utley & Co., Niagara Falls,
Upper Canada. Original tablet.
Ca. 1860 . . . .$2000.00

8

SETH THOMAS 8-DAY WEIGHT
DRIVEN COLUMN CLOCK.
On paper "Patterson, Toronto,
Canada West." Mottled "marble"
columns, mirror in middle panel.
Ca. 1860' Ht. 36"   . . $750.00

SETH THOMAS 8-DAY STRIKE.
Label — "J.M. Patterson, Toronto,
Canada West." Empire case, rose-
wood veneer. Ht. 32" . . $975.00

SETH THOMAS 30-HOUR.
With hour strike. On paper —
"J.M. Patterson, Hamilton,
Canada West."
Solid mahogany case with
mahogany veneer.
Ca. 1855.
Ht. 25" $425.00

Above — Left —
SETH THOMAS UMBRIA
8-day with strike, spring wound.
on dial — "Seifert, Quebec" —
a silversmith who sold his business
to Birks.
Walnut case. Ca. 1905. . . $1250.00

Above — Right —
REGULATOR.
8-day French pin whell movement.
Ash case made in Canada by
Counter, Seaforth, Ontario.
Ht. 6' 6" 3500.00

Left —
SETH THOMAS REGULATOR.
"Seth Thomas Clock Co., Plymouth
Hollow" on pendulum, also on clock
paper. 8-day time only with two
weights. Seconds hand missing.
Rosewood veneer case. "Angus
McFee, Belleville" on dial.
Ca. 1870.
Ht. 41" Dial diam. 20" . . 1500.00

The
Arthur Pequegnat Clock Co.,

Berlin (Kitchener), Ontario. 1903 - 1942

. . . ."Canada's Only Clock Makers.". . . . . ."We are satisfied that if a careful comparison is made of "Pequegnat Clocks" with competing lines, the result will prove very much to our advantage for even a hurried inspection cannot fail to convince that in construction our movements are unexcelled, while in workmanship and finish Pequegnat Clock movements are vastly superior, and our clock cases are much more substantially constructed."

From Arthur Pequegnat Clock Co., 1918 catalogue.

Arthur Pequegnat, a Swiss clockmaker, who arrived in Canada with his family in 1874, opened his clock company in Berlin, now Kitchener, Ontario in 1903. His aim was to manufacture Canadian made clocks at prices competitive with American imports. His clocks proved to be very popular, the Arthur Pequegnat Clock Company produced wall, shelf and grandfather clocks and over 90 models of clocks were listed and illustrated in their catalogues. The factory remained in production until 1942, when because of the war, shortages of raw materials, such as brass, forced closure of the business.

Pequegnat clocks have 8-day movements except for "Moncton" and "Regina" which are 15-day time-only clocks with double spring movements. "Regulator No. 1" is the only weight driven model, an 8-day time-only clock with a Graham dead beat escapement. Most of the shelf clocks have hour and half-hour strike, many striking the half-hour on a separate bell. The kitchen and wall clocks strike hours only on a cathedral gong.

Many Pequegnat clocks were offered with a selection of features, e.g. time, time and strike or time and strike with calendar. These alternatives were not offered in all models, however, "Brandon," "Canadian Time" and "King Edward" were available with any of the combinations offered.

Wood cases were individually made, originally at the Berlin Interior Hardwood Co. until 1920 when Arthur Pequegnat bought a factory in Breslau, Ontario to produce cases for his clocks. The majority of cases were made of quarter cut oak, with a variety of finishes, such as walnut, mahogany, golden oak, fumed oak, weathered oak or old English. Cases made of mahogany or walnut woods were available in some models or by special order and cases made of maple and other woods have been found.

Case styles remained constant during the four decades of production, however, slight modifications were made on some models and sometimes Pequegnat clock cases are not exactly as illustrated and described in the catalogues.

ORNAMENTAL ACCESSORIES USED BY
THE ARTHUR PEQUEGNAT CLOCK COMPANY

Pressed wood — Beaver
             — Gingerbread style in kitchen clocks.
Turned finials and pillars.
Canadian decorative themes: Beaver; Fleur-De-Lis; Maple Leaves.
Inlay
Applied carving and moulding.
Columns with plain or elaborate capitals and bases.
Lion's mask.
Rococo style metal feet; turned wood feet. Ornamental feet made of composition and matching the colour of the case were used by the Arthur Pequegnat Clock Company towards the end of their time of production.
Decals — of King Edward; Maple Leaves; Canadian Time; inlay and dials.
Doors on grandfather clocks   — Chipped glass — pebbled finish at edges.
                                 — Bevelled glass.
Bevelled glass was also used on some shelf clocks.
Iron case — Premier model.

BEZELS, DIALS & NUMERALS

Glazed door or frame over dial, e.g. wall clocks, grandfather clocks.
Mission — Applied cast brass numerals or decals, e.g. "Dominion" or "Nelson"
Types of Dial — Paper on tin; painted metal; celluloid/Ivorine; porcelain or enamel; soft porcelain; silvered.
Hands   — Fleur-De-Lis, e.g. "Ontario"
               Solid Spade, e.g. "Daisy"
               Pierced Spade, e.g. "Brandon"
               Pierced Diamond Shape, e.g. "Vernon"
Numerals — Arabic; Roman.

VARIANTS

Clocks are sometimes found that are basically as described and illustrated in the Arthur Pequegnat catalogues, but with a variation. An example of this is the "King Edward" model which is identical to the catalogue model except it has a "Canadian Time" glass. Another "King Edward" has been found with the two mainspring "Moncton" movement. There are clocks with altered labels and clocks which are not listed in catalogues. Uncatalogued Pequegnat models are illustrated in this section.

Other Pequegnat clocks, for special occasions or purposes, were made on a "one-only" basis, with regular standard movements or a modified movement. The Pequegnat Clock Company advertised and sold movements for clocks, so it is possible to find clocks in cases not made for the Arthur Pequegnat Clock Company.

PEQUEGNAT CLOCKS

The values quoted in this section are intended as a guide only — the condition of the movement, case and dial etc. have a strong influence on the price of a Pequegnat clock.

Clocks with "Berlin" on the label and dial are generally of higher value than their "Kitchener" counterpart.

The range in values quoted is intended to cover these situations.

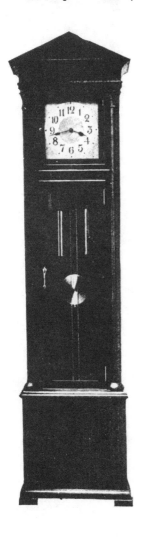

ALBERTA.
8-day weight movement, brass weights, double strike on tuned rods.
Also came with imported Westminster chime movement.
Ht. 82" W. 21¼"
Case: Golden oak, fumed oak, walnut or mahogany.
Bevelled glass in doors.
Also —
Mahogany or quarter oak with applied cast brass numerals.
Bevelled glass in door.

$2000.00 - $3000.00

HALIFAX.
8-day weight movement, brass
weights, double strike on tuned rods.
Ht. 80" W. 22¼"
Case: Golden oak, fumed oak,
walnut or mahogany.
Bevelled glass in doors.
Also —
Mahogany or quarter oak with
applied cast brass numerals.
Bevelled glass in door.
$1500.00 - $2500.00

PEQUEGNAT GRANDFATHER
CLOCK.
Uncatalogued, name not known
for this clock.
8-day weight movement with
strike.
Ht. 82" W. 19"
Case: Mahogany or medium oak.
Brass dial, black numerals.
$2200.00 - $3000.00

LEADER.
8-day weight movement, brass
weights. Time and strike.
Ht. 76" W. 22¼"
Case: Weathered oak.
Applied cast brass numerals.
Chipped glass in doors.
$1500.00 - $2300.00

VANCOUVER.
8-day weight movement, brass
weights, cathedral gong.
Ht. 75¼" W. 20"
Case: Weathered oak or fumed
oak. Applied cast brass numerals.
Chipped glass in door.
$2000.00 - $3000.00

CHIPPED GLASS: Pebbled finish at edges.

NELSON.
8-day weight movement, brass weights, double strike on tuned rods.
Ht. 81" W. 22½"
Case: Golden oak, fumed oak or mahogany.
Applied cast brass numerals.
Bevelled glass in door.
$2000.00 - $3000.00

VERNON.
8-day weight movement, brass weights, cathedral gong. Also came with double strike movement and Westminster chime movement.
Ht. 80" W. 22¼"
Case: Fumed oak or golden oak.
Applied cast brass numerals.
Chipped glass in door.
$2000.00 - $3000.00

CANADA.
8-day weight movement, brass weights, cathedral gong. Also came with double strike movement or Westminster chime movement.
Ht. 74" W. 18¼"
Case: Mission style, fumed oak or weathered oak.
Applied cast brass numerals.
$800.00 - $1200.00

PEQUEGNAT GRANDFATHER CLOCK.
Uncatalogued, name not known for this clock. Case similar to Canada model.
8-day spring wound movement with strike.
Ht. 72"
Case: Mission style, golden oak.
Applied cast brass numerals.
$800.00 - $1200.00

Above — Left —
BEAVER SPECIAL.
8-day, strike on rods.
Porcelain dial.
Ht. 35¼" W. 14"
Case: Golden oak or
mahogany finish.
$2500.00 - $3500.00

Above — Right —
BEAVER.
8-day, strike on rods.
Ht. 31½" W. 13½"
Case: Golden oak or
mahogany finish.
$1600.00 - $2500.00

Below — Left —
WALL CLOCK.
Movement marked
"Pequegnat, Berlin."
8-day bim-bam strike,
hours and half-hours.
Dial marked "Franco-
American Clock Co.,
Toronto."
Ht. 45" W. 17"
Case: Maple.
$595.00

Above — Left & Right —
MONCTON.
15-day, time only, two mainspring
Graham deadbeat escapement.
Ht. 34½" W. 16"
Case: Golden oak, fumed oak or
mahogany finish.
$ 900.00 - $1400.00

Below — Left —
REGULATOR NO. 1
8-day weight, time, 80 beat
movement, Graham deadbeat
escapement. Lantern pinions,
maintaining power, brass weight.
Brass pendulum ball, wood rod.
Ht. 36" W. 16"
Case: Golden oak or mahogany
finish.
$2000.00 - $3000.00

KING EDWARD
Brass Bezel

KING EDWARD
Wood Frame

KING EDWARD.
Illustrated — 8-day, time only.
Ht. 30" W. 16"
The King Edward model also came
with —
    Strike movement
    Time and calendar movement
    Strike and calendar movement.
Case: Golden oak, fumed oak or
weathered oak.

Brass Bezel $1100.00 - $1250.00
Wood Frame $ 900.00 - $1100.00

KING EDWARD
Canadian Time glass

Above — Left —
BRANDON.
Illustrated — 8-day, time only with
calendar. Ht. 26¾" W. 16"
The Brandon model also came
with —
    Time movement
    Strike movement
    Strike and calendar movement.
Case: Golden oak or fumed oak.
$500.00 - $750.00

Above — Right —
REGINA.
15-day, two mainsprings,
Graham deadbeat escapement.
Ht. 32½" W. 16"
Case: Golden oak, fumed oak
or mahogany finish.
$2200.00 - $3000.00

Below — Left —
PRESTON.
8-day, time and strike. Also
came with 8-day time only
movement.
Ht. 19½" W. 12"
Case: Golden oak finish.
$450.00 - $700.00

21

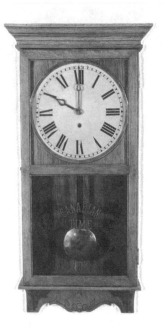

CANADIAN TIME.
Illustrated — 8-day, time only.
Ht. 36" W. 18"
The Canadian Time model also came with —
    Strike movement
    Time and calendar movement
    Strike and calendar movement.
Case: Golden oak, fumed oak or weathered oak.
$500.00 - $700.00

IDEAL.
Illustrated — 8-day, time and strike, cathedral gong. Also came with 8-day time only movement.
Dial decorated with a maple leaf at each corner.
Ht. 24" W. 11"
Case: Oak finish, mahogany finish or walnut finish.
$350.00 - $500.00

YORK.
8-day time only. Also came with 8-day time and strike movement.
16½" x 16½"
Case: Golden oak, mahogany or walnut finish.
$1200.00 - $1800.00

KINGSTON.
8-day striking movement.
Applied cast brass numerals.
Ht. 32" W. 15"
Case: Weathered oak.
$500.00 - $750.00

OTTAWA.
8-day, hour and ½-hour strike,
cathedral gong. Applied cast
brass numerals. Ht. 32½" W. 15"
Case: Fumed oak or weathered
oak.
$500.00 - $750.00

DAISY.
8-day, time only.
Ht. 16¼" W. 8¼"
Two case styles:
mahogany finish
or walnut finish.
$450.00 - $650.00

TORONTO. Illustrated — 8-day, time only. Also came with time
and strike movement. Diam. 16¼"
Case: Golden oak or mahogany finish. . . . . . .$400.00 - $500.00

WINDSOR. 8-day, time only. Plain shelf. Length 39"
Case: Weathered oak or fumed oak. $1100.00 - $1600.00

WOODSTOCK. 8-day, time only. Shelf with plate rail. Length 39"
Case: Fumed oak or golden oak. . . . . $1200.00 - $2000.00

Above — Left —
MONARCH. Round Top.
8-day, time and strike.
Ht. 24½" W. 18½"
Case: Golden oak.
$500.00 - $600.00

Above — Right —
MONARCH. Slant Top.
Maple leaf glass.
8-day, time and strike.
Ht. 25" W. 18"
$500.00 - $600.00

Below — Left —
CANUCK.
8-day, time and strike,
cathedral gong.
Ht. 22" W. 14"
Case: Golden oak.
$300.00 - $400.00

MAPLE LEAF. 8-day, time and strike, cathedral gong. Ht. 22½"
Case: Golden oak or walnut finish.   . . . . $325.00 - $400.00
NOTE: The Maple Leaf kitchen clock came in five case styles.
The other style is similar to the case above, left, but with a
steeple type top.

Above — Left —
BELLEVILLE.
8-day, strike on gong.
Applied cast brass numerals.
Ht. 22" W. 16¼"
Case: Weathered oak.
$450.00 - $650.00

Above — Right —
TOKIO.
8-day, time and strike,
cathedral gong.
Applied cast brass numerals.
Ht. 19¼" W. 9½"
Case: Weathered oak.
$300.00 - $400.00

Below — Left —
MIDGET.
8-day, time only.
Applied cast brass numerals.
Ht. 17" W. 8¼"
Case: Weathered oak.
$225.00 - $325.00

Above — Left —
QUEBEC.
8-day, time and strike.
Applied cast brass numerals.
Ht. 20" W. 13"
Case: Golden oak.
$250.00 - $400.00

Above — Right —
BRANTFORD.
8-day, strike on gong.
Applied cast brass numerals.
Ht. 24" W. 16¼"
Case: Weathered oak.
$300.00 - $450.00

Below — Left —
MONTREAL.
8-day, time and strike,
cathedral gong.
Applied cast brass numerals.
Ht. 20" W. 13"
Case: Weathered oak.
$250.00 - $400.00

MILTON.
8-day, time and strike, cathedral
gong. Ht. 14½" W. 10½"
Case: Golden oak, fumed oak or
mahogany.
$300.00 - $400.00

SARNIA.
8-day, time and strike, cathedral gong.
Also came with double strike movement and tuned rods. Ht. 16½" W. 12½"
Case: Golden oak, fumed oak or
walnut.
$400.00 - $550.00

WINNIPEG.
8-day, time and strike, cathedral
gong. Ht. 17" W. 12½"
Case: Inlaid mahogany, bright or
satin finish.
$500.00 - $800.00

CHATHAM.
8-day, time and strike, cathedral gong.
Also came with double strike movement and tuned rods. Ht. 16" W. 13"
Case: Golden oak, fumed oak,
mahogany or walnut.
$350.00 - $500.00

VICTORIA.
8-day, time and strike, cathedral
gong. Also came with double strike
movement and tuned rods.
Ht. 16½" W. 13 3/8"
Case: Golden oak, fumed oak or
mahogany.
$400.00 - $550.00

PETERBOROUGH — LATE.
8-day, time and strike, cathedral
gong. Also came with double strike
movement and tuned rods.
Ht. 11" W. 13"
Case: Golden oak, fumed oak or
weathered oak.
$300.00 - $400.00

Left —
PEQUEGNAT SHELF CLOCK.
Uncatalogued.
8-day, time and strike.
"Berlin" on dial.
Ht. 12" W. 10½"
Case: Golden oak.
$400.00 - $600.00

Right —
PANTHEON.
8-day, time and strike, cathedral
gong. Also came with double
strike movement and tuned rods.
Ht. 13½" W. 18"
Case: Golden oak, fumed oak or
walnut.
$350.00 - $500.00

Above — Left —
ST. THOMAS
8-day, time and strike.
Applied cast brass numerals.
Ht. 21½" W. 13"
Case: Golden oak.
$500.00 - $650.00

Above — Right —
HAMILTON — TALL.
8-day, time and strike,
cathedral gong.
Ht. 21½" W. 13"
Case: Golden oak.
$400.00 - $600.00

Below — Left —
CITADEL.
8-day, time and strike,
cathedral gong.
Applied cast brass numerals.
Ht. 25¼" W. 16"
Case: Quarter cut oak, golden
finish with bevelled glass.
$800.00 - $1000.00

PARIS.
8-day, hour and ½-hour strike,
cathedral gong.
Ht. 14¼" W. 10¾"
Case: Inlaid mahogany with
bright or satin finish.
$700.00 - $1000.00

PICTON.
8-day, time and strike, cathedral
gong.
Ht. 14½" W. 10¾"
Case: Golden oak, fumed oak or
walnut.
$300.00 $450.00

BEDFORD.
8-day, hour and ½-hour strike,
cathedral gong. Porcelain or
silvered dial. Ht. 9¾" W. 8¾"
Case: Mahogany, golden oak
or fumed oak.
$150.00 - $250.00

BONNIE.
8-day, hour and ½-hour strike,
cathedral gong.
Ht. 10 5/8"
Three styles of case, golden oak.
$250.00 - $350.00

PANTHENON. 8-day, strikes hour on gong, ½-hour on bell. Ht. 13" W. 17"
Case: Quarter cut oak. . . . . $350.00 - $500.00

AMHERST. 8-day, hour and ½-hour strike, cathedral gong. Also came with
double strike movement and tuned rods. Ht. 16¾" W. 11½"
Case: Golden oak or fumed oak. . . . . $250.00 - $400.00

COLONIAL. 8-day, strikes hour on gong, ½-hour on bell. Ht. 10½" W. 15¾"
Case: Golden oak. . . . . $300.00 - $400.00

Left —
JEWEL.
8-day, strikes hour on
gong, ½-hour on bell.
Ht. 10" W. 12½"
Case: Golden oak.
$250.00 - $350.00

Right —
GUELPH.
8-day, strikes hour on
gong, ½-hour on bell.
Ht. 10¾" W. 13"
Case: Quarter cut oak,
golden finish, gilt or
bronzed fittings.
$250.00 - $350.00

Right —
LONDON.
8-day, strikes hour on
gong, ½-hour on bell.
Ht. 11½" W. 17"
Case: Quarter cut oak,
golden finish. Gilt or
bronzed fittings.
$300.00 $425.00

Left —
STRATFORD.
8-day, hour and ½-hour
strike, two rod strike
available.
Ht. 11½" W. 17"
Case: Polished black.
$300.00 - $450.00

Right —
BERLIN.
8-day, strikes hour on
gong, ½-hour on bell.
Ht. 11" W. 15½"
Case: Golden oak,
weathered oak, forest
green or imitation
mahogany. Gilt or
bronzed fittings.
$275.00 - $400.00

Left —
ONTARIO
8-day, strikes hour on
gong, ½-hour on bell.
Case: Mahogany, golden
or weathered oak, forest
green, or black with
marbleized mouldings.
Gilt or bronzed fittings.
$325.00 - $425.00

Left —
SIMCOE.
8-day, strikes hour on
gong, ½-hour on bell.
Ht. 10¾" W. 14"
Case: Quarter cut oak,
golden finish. Gilt or
bronzed fittings.
$250.00 - $350.00

Right —
GRECIAN.
8-day, strikes hour on
gong, ½-hour on bell.
Ht. 11½" W. 17¾"
Case: Mahogany, golden
or weathered oak, forest
green or black with
marbleized mouldings.
Gilt or Bronzed
fittings.
$300.00 - $425.00

WARD.
8-day, time and strike, cathedral
gong. Ht. 11" W. 10¼"
Case: Golden oak or fumed oak.
$200.00 - $275.00

SOO.
8-day, time and strike, cathedral
gong. Ht. 10" W. 10½"
Case: Golden oak or fumed oak.
Also came in case with straight sides.
$200.00 - $300.00

PEQUEGNAT SHELF CLOCKS — NOT SHOWN

BARRIE. 8-day, strikes hour on gong, half-hour on bell. Ht. 10¾" W. 13"
Case: Quarter cut oak, golden finish. Gilt or bronzed fittings.
$200.00 - $325.00

BIJOU. 8-day, strikes hour on gong, half-hour on bell. Ht. 10" W. 11½"
Case: Golden oak.
$200.00 - $300.00

BRAMPTON. 8-day, strikes hour and half-hour, cathedral gong. Also
came with double strike on two tuned rods. Ht. 11¼" W. 15½"
Case: Golden oak, fumed oak or walnut finish.
$300.00 - $450.00

CHESTER. Uncatalogued model. Case and numeral style reminiscent of
Art Deco style with metal bezal and chapter ring, keyhole hands. Ca. 1940.
$150.00 - $250.00

DOMINION. 8-day, strikes hour and half-hour, cathedral gong. Ht. 10 5/8"
Three styles of case: golden oak.
$250.00 - $350.00

ELITE. 8-day, time and strike, cathedral gong. Porcelain dial. Ht. 9¾"
W. 8½" Case: Mahogany, golden oak or fumed oak.
$200.00 - $300.00

GALT. 8-day, strikes hour on gong, half-hour on bell. Ht. 10¾" W. 14"
Case: Quarter cut oak, golden finish. Gilt or bronzed fittings.
$200.00 - $300.00

HAMILTON — WIDE. 8-day, strikes hour and half-hour, cathedral gong.
Also came with double chime strike. Ht. 11½" W. 15½"
Case: Golden oak.
$300.00 - $400.00

LINDSAY. 8-day, time and strike, cathedral gong. Ht. 14½" W. 10½"
Case: Similar to Milton, but with a triangular pediment. Quarter cut oak.
$300.00 - $400.00

PANTHEON B. 8-day, double strike on two tuned rods. Ht. 13" W. 17"
Case: Golden oak, fumed oak or walnut finish.
$250.00 - $400.00

PETERBOROUGH — EARLY. 8-day, time and strike, cathedral gong.
Ht. 11" W. 13" Case: Similar to Soo, but with four columns. Golden oak
or weathered oak. Gilt or bronzed fittings.
$300.00 - $425.00

PREMIER. 8-day, strikes hour on gong, half-hour on bell. Ht. 10½" W. 14"
Case: Black enamelled iron.
$350.00 - $550.00

Left —
CAPITOL.
8-day, double strike on two
tuned rods. Ht. 9 3/8" W. 21"
Case: Mahogany or walnut.
$150.00 - $250.00

Right —
MAJESTIC.
Uncatalogued model.
8-day, time and strike.
Case: Mahogany with
inlay decal.
$250.00 - $350.00

Left —
OXFORD.
8-day, time and strike,
cathedral gong.
Porcelain dial.
Ht. 10 7/8" W. 17¼"
Case: Mahogany, walnut,
golden oak or fumed oak.
$250.00 $350.00

Right —
GUELPH B.
8-day, time and strike,
cathedral gong.
Porcelain dial.
Ht. 10¼" W. 20"
Case: Mahogany, walnut,
golden oak or fumed oak.
$250.00 - $350.00

Left —
ORILLIA.
8-day, hour and ½-hour
strike, cathedral gong.
Ht. 10 7/8" W. 17¼"
Case: Mahogany, walnut,
golden oak or fumed oak.
$200.00 - $300.00

Right —
SHERBROOKE.
8-day, time and strike, cathedral
gong. Porcealin dial.
Ht. 10 7/8" W. 17¼"
Case: Mahogany, walnut, golden
oak or fumed oak.
$250.00 - $350.00

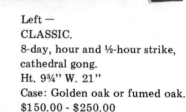

Left —
CLASSIC.
8-day, hour and ½-hour strike,
cathedral gong.
Ht. 9¾" W. 21"
Case: Golden oak or fumed oak.
$150.00 - $250.00

Right —
SWAN.
8-day, hour and ½-hour strike,
cathedral gong.
Ht. 10¼" W. 19½"
Case: Mahogany finish, walnut
finish, golden oak or fumed oak.
$150.00 - $250.00

PEQUEGNAT TAMBOUR CLOCKS — NOT SHOWN

BEAUTY. 8-day, hour and half-hour strike, cathedral gong. Also came with double strike on two tuned rods. Ht. 10" W. 17¾" Case: Mahogany finish or walnut finish.
$150.00 $250.00

DANDY. 8-day, hour and half-hour strike, cathedral gong. Also came with double strike on two tuned rods. Ht. 9 3/8" W. 21" Case: Mahogany finish or walnut finish.
$250.00 - $250.00

DELIGHT. 8-day, hour and half-hour strike, cathedral gong. Also came with double strike on two tuned rods. Ht. 9 7/8" W. 22" Case: Mahogany finish or walnut finish.
$150.00 - $250.00

ECLIPSE. 8-day, hour and half-hour strike, cathedral gong. Ht. 9¾" W. 20¾" Case: Golden oak, fumed oak, mahogany finish or walnut finish.
$250.00 - $350.00

ESSEX. Uncatalogued model, case style similar to Majestic. 8-day, time and strike.
$250.00 - $350.00

LONDON B. 8-day, hour and half-hour strike, cathedral gong. Also came with double strike on two tuned rods. Ht. 10½" W. 20¼" Case: Mahogany, golden oak or fumed oak.
$200.00 $300.00

ROYAL. 8-day, hour and half-hour strike, cathedral gong. Ht. 9¾" W. 21" Case: Golden oak, fumed oak, mahogany finish or walnut finish.
$150.00 - $300.00

SUPREME. 8-day, hour and half-hour strike, cathedral gong. Ht. 9¾" W. 22½" Case: Walnut.
$250.00 - $350.00

SYDNEY. 8-day, hour and half-hour strike, cathedral gong. Porcelain dial. Ht. 10¾" W. 16" Case: Walnut, mahogany, golden oak or fumed oak.
$250.00 - $350.00

VICTOR. Uncatalogued model, case shape similar to Capitol, with decal that looks like inlay below dial.
$150.00 - $250.00

VOGUE. Uncatalogued model, case style similar in shape to Classic, sometimes found with a decal below the dial.
$150.00 - $250.00

AMERICAN CLOCKS

Above — Left —
WOOD WORKS 30-HOUR CLOCK.
By Jerome & Darrow, Bristol, Conn.
Wood dial, all original. Ca. 1820.
Ht. 33½" $995.00

Above — Right —
WOOD WORKS 30-HOUR STRIKE.
By Boardman & Wells, Bristol, Conn.
Stencilled columns and splat, original
mirror. Ht. 31" 495.00

Left —
30-HOUR WEIGHT DRIVEN
"LOOKING GLASS" CLOCK. With
strike. By Williams, Orton & Prestons,
Conn. 415.00

Above — Left —
FOUR COLUMN 30-HOUR SHELF
CLOCK. By Sperry & Shaw, N.Y.
Ca. 1848. Ht. 26¼" . . . . $ 495.00

Above — Right —
30-HOUR STRIKING CLOCK. Brass
movement and fusee. By Smith &
Goderich, Bristol, Conn. Rosewood
veneer case, original tablet and glass,
painted tin dial.
Ca. 1847.- 52. Ht. 16½"
Rare 850.00

Left —
CALENDAR CLOCK. Manufactured
for National Clock Co. by New Haven
Clock Co. 8-day with hour strike,
mahogany case. Ca. 1890.
Ht. 26¾" 2000.00

OGEE 8-DAY STRIKE CLOCK. By E.N. Welch. Rosewood veneer case, original tablet — the Capitol at Albany, N.Y. Ca. 1848. Ht. 29" $400.00

30-HOUR OGEE. By Wm. L. Gilbert. Original condition. Ca. 1870. Ht. 25½" $325.00

MINIATURE OGEE. 30-hour, spring wound. By E.N. Welch. Mahogany veneer case, new dial, original glass. Ht. 18¼" $275.00

WATERBURY OGEE CLOCK. 30-hour strike. Veneer stripped, new hands, original tablet. Ca. 1875. Ht. 20" $200.00

Above — Left —
STEEPLE CLOCK. By Chauncey Jerome. 30-hour fusee movement, hour strike. Mahogany veneer case. Made for the English market — Trafalgar Square scene on door. Ht. 20" $750.00

Above — Right —
STEEPLE CLOCK. Made and sold by A.J. Taylor, 105 John St., New York. 8-day, hour strike, original tablet. Ca. 1867-70.
Ht. 20" 295.00

Left —
WATERBURY STEEPLE CLOCK. 30-hour, strike on gong. Walnut veneer case, dial and tablet restored. Ca. 1855. Ht. 19¾" 245.00

Above — Left —
STEEPLE CLOCK. By E.C.
Brewster & Son. 8-day strike.
Rosewood veneer case, all
original including tablet.
Ht. 19½" 325.00

Above — Right —
NEW HAVEN STEEPLE CLOCK.
8-day with strike and alarm.
Rosewood veneer case, original
tablet, new paper dial.
Ca. 1870. Ht. 20½" .. 300.00

Left —
ANSONIA STEEPLE CLOCK.
30-hour with strike. Mahogany
veneer case, tablet not original.
Ht. 19" 235.00

SETH THOMAS PILLAR CLOCK. 8-day with strike. Mahogany veneer, original tablet. Ht. 17½" $450.00

JEROME BEEHIVE CLOCK. 8-day, hour strike. Mahogany veneer, original tablet. Ht. 19" $395.00

BEEHIVE CLOCK. Manufactured by Terhune & Bottsford, New York. 8-day, hour strike. Tablet not original. Ht. 19" $295.00

WILLIAM L. GILBERT DORIC. 8-day, hour strike. Cherry veneer case, original tablet. Ca. 1860. Ht. 17" $445.00

COTTAGE CLOCK. Jerome & Co. "Dreadnought" with original label. Pat'd. Feb. 11, 1879. 30-hour, time only. Ht. 14" $245.00

COTTAGE CLOCK. By Welch, Spring & Co. 8-day with strike. Mahogany veneer case, new dial. Ht. 18" $295.00

NEW HAVEN COTTAGE CLOCK. 8-day, strike on gong. Mahogany veneer case. Original tablet. Ht. 15½" $325.00

SETH THOMAS COTTAGE CLOCK. Lyre movement, 8-day with strike. Mahogany veneer, original tablet. Ht. 14" $350.00

COTTAGE CLOCK. Maker
unknown. 30-hour, time
only. Oak case.
Ht. 11" $225.00

COTTAGE CLOCK. By
Wm. L. Gilbert. 30-hour
with strike and alarm.
Rosewood veneer case.
Ca. 1866 - 71.
Ht. 13½" $275.00

JEROME COTTAGE CLOCK.
8-day strike. Rosewood veneer
case, original tablet. Ca. 1870.
Ht. 13¼" $285.00

NEW HAVEN COTTAGE
CLOCK. 8-day, brass movement
with strike. Rosewood veneer
case, painted dial, original
tablet. Ca. 1875.
Ht. 13½" $315.00

48

Above — Left —
MIRROR CLOCK. By Wm. L.
Gilbert Clock Co. Occidental
model. 8-day, hour strike.
Ca. 1870. Ht. 23½" $500.00

Above — Right —
ANSONIA MIRROR CLOCK.
8-day with strike and alarm.
Ht. 23½" 500.00

Left —
NEW HAVEN MIRROR CLOCK.
8-day with strike, regulating dial
pendulum. Mahogany case.
All original.
Ht. 24" 525.00

ANSONIA TEAR DROP CLOCK.
8-day with strike, pseudo mercury
pendulum. Mahogany case.
Ht. 23" $365.00

LIBERTY PARLOUR CLOCK. By
Charles F. Adams, Erie, Penn. 8-day
strike with calendar. Walnut case.
Ht. 22" $525.00

SHELF CLOCK. Maker unknown.
8-day with alarm. Walnut case,
original glass. Ht. 22" . .$345.00

SETH THOMAS SHELF CLOCK.
8-day strike. Carved solid walnut
case. Ht. 19" $425.00

Above — Left —
WATERBURY SHELF CLOCK.
8-day strike. Mahogany case.
Ht. 20" $325.00

Above — Right —
ANSONIA SHELF CLOCK.
8-day with strike. Dark walnut
case with decorative gallery.
Ht. 18½" 375.00

Left —
SETH THOMAS SHELF CLOCK.
8-day with strike. Rosewood
veneer case. Ht. 15½" . . 450.00

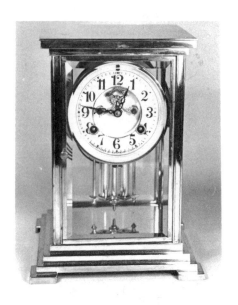

Above — Left —
CRYSTAL REGULATOR.
Waterbury Clock Co., Ca. 1900.
8-day, hour strike, porcelain dial,
bevelled glass in brass case.
Ht. 9" $650.00

Above — Right —
CRYSTAL REGULATOR.
Seth Thomas, Ca. 1910.
8-day, hour and ½-hour strike.
Bevelled glass in brass case.
Ht. 9½" 795.00

Left —
CRYSTAL REGULATOR.
Seth Thomas. 8-day with strike.
Bevelled glass in brass case.
Ht. 10" 750.00

SESSIONS GINGERBREAD CLOCK.
8-day strike. Original condition.
Ht. 23" $335.00

INGRAHAM GINGERBREAD
CLOCK. 8-day strike on gong.
Ht. 21½" $295.00

SMALL GINGERBREAD CLOCK.
Maker unknown. 8-day, strike on
gong. Dial not original.
Ht. 15½" $195.00

WATERBURY GINGERBREAD
CLOCK. Unaka model. 8-day,
½-hour strike. Oak case.
Ht. 17" $350.00

ANSONIA GINGERBREAD CLOCK. 8-day, ½-hour strike. Walnut finish. Ca. 1895. Ht. 22½" $295.00

SETH THOMAS GINGERBREAD CLOCK. 8-day with stop work and hour strike. Walnut case. All original. Ht. 21½" . . $315.00

GINGERBREAD CLOCK. By Welch Clock Co. 8-day with alarm. Walnut case, all original. Ca. 1890. Ht. 15½" $295.00

NEW HAVEN GINGERBREAD CLOCK. 1-day, hour strike on gong. 1880's. Ht. 19" $275.00

ANSONIA GINGERBREAD CLOCK.
8-day strike. Walnut case. Pat'd 1882.
Ht. 22½" $350.00

WATERBURY GINGERBREAD
CLOCK. 8-day with strike. All
original. Ht. 21½" . . . $315.00

ANSONIA GINGERBREAD CLOCK.
Berkley model. 8-day, hour strike. All
original, case restored. $340.00

ANSONIA GINGERBREAD CLOCK.
Australia model. 8-day, strike on gong.
Walnut case. Ht. 21" . . . $395.00

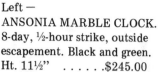

Left —
ANSONIA MARBLE CLOCK.
8-day, ½-hour strike, outside
escapement. Black and green.
Ht. 11½" $245.00

Right —
INGRAHAM ALDINE MODEL.
8-day, ½-hour strike. Black
marbleized wood case.
Ca. 1890. Ht. 10" . .$195.00

Left —
SESSIONS MANTEL
CLOCK. 8-day, ½-hour
strike. Black wood
with green marbleized
trim. Ca. 1900.
Ht. 11¼" . . $150.00

Right —
SETH THOMAS
MANTEL CLOCK.
8-day, strikes hour
on gong, ½-hour on
bell. Marbleized wood
case. Ht. 11¾" $215.00

Above — Left —
SETH THOMAS MANTEL CLOCK.
8-day with strike. Porcelain dial,
inlaid case. Sold by Henry Birks &
Sons Ltd. Ca. 1900.
Ht. 10" $200.00

Above — Right —
SETH THOMAS MANTEL CLOCK.
8-day, ½-hour strike.
Ht. 10" 285.00

Left —
LIBRARY OR OFFICE CLOCK.
Make unknown. 8-day, strike on
gong. Solid walnut case.
Ht. 16" 325.00

Right —
WALTHAM TIMEPIECE.
8-day balance movement.
Winds from underneath.
Ca. 1920.
Ht. 11" $185.00

Above — Left —
BANJO CLOCK. 8-day timepiece by E. Howard
& Co., Boston, Mass. Cherry case with rosewood
graining. Ca. 1880. Ht. 29" $3000.00

Above — Centre —
NEW HAVEN BANJO CLOCK. 8-day with strike.
Mahogany veneer case, nautical theme on tablets.
Ca. 1920's. Ht. 34" 1000.00

Above — Right —
SESSIONS BANJO CLOCK. 8-day pendulum
movement with strike. Birch case, walnut
finish. Ht. 31" 795.00

Left —
NEW HAVEN MINIATURE BANJO CLOCK.
8-day, time only. Burl walnut case.
Ca. 1910. . . . . 395.00

Left —
SETH THOMAS
REGULATOR NO. 31.
Last railroad clock before
electrics.
Ht. 60" $3650.00

Right —
WALTHAM
REGULATOR MODEL 13.
8-day, mercury pendulum.
Oak case. All original.
From Maine Central
Railroad station,
Portland. 3500.00

Left —
SETH THOMAS
REGULATOR NO. 2.
Time only, with book weight.
Made by E.N. Welch & Co.
under contract for Seth
Thomas, 1878 - 79.
Ht. 33" $1450.00

Right —
NEW HAVEN REGULATOR.
8-day, weight driven, time
only. Oak case.
Ht. 33" 950.00

SETH THOMAS REGULATOR. 30-day, time only. Double mainspring. Oak case. ht. 40" $1350.00

SESSIONS REGULATOR. Timepiece with calendar. Ht. 36" $535.00

GILBERT REGULATOR. 8-day time-piece with calendar. Refinished oak case, new dial. Ht. 27½" . . $495.00

ANSONIA MODEL A LONG DROP REGULATOR. 8-day, hour strike. Walnut case, original paper. 1885 - 1900. Ht. 32" $600.00

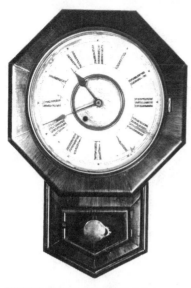

NEW HAVEN SCHOOL ROOM
CLOCK. 8-day, time only.
Ca. 1875.
Diam. of dial 12"   . . $350.00

ANSONIA SCHOOL ROOM
CLOCK. 8-day strike. Walnut
case. Ht. 30" $465.00

SESSIONS MINIATURE SCHOOL
ROOM TIMEPIECE. 8-day. Oak
case. All original. Early 1900's.
Ht. 19" $395.00

SETH THOMAS "NEW WORLD."
15-day, two mainspring, time only.
Oak case. Ht. 31" $1200.00

SESSIONS MINIATURE DROP
OCTAGON. Fulton model. 1912-
17. 8-day, hour and ½-hour strike.
Oak case. Ht. 19½" . . $425.00

WATERBURY OCTAGONAL WALL
CLOCK. 8-day, lever escapement.
Ca. 1890. Diam. 8½" $225.00

ANSONIA WALL CLOCK. 8-day
strike, cherry frame.
Diam. 17½" $395.00

Above —
NEW HAVEN WALL CLOCK.
30-day, 2 mainsprings. Ca. 1900.
Oak frame.
Diam. of dial 18" . . $495.00

Right —
ANSONIA WALL CLOCK.
8-day, hour and ½-hour strike.
Replacement dial. Walnut frame.
Diam. 16" 345.00

Above — Left —
ANGLO/AMERICAN CLOCK.
8-day American movement with
strike. British walnut case with
various wood inlays. Ca. 1885.
Ht. 27" $560.00

Above — Right —
ANGLO/AMERICAN CLOCK.
8-day New Haven movement
with hour and ½-hour strike.
Inlaid walnut veneer case.
Ca. 1885. .
Diam. of dial 12"   . . 595.00

Left —
ANGLO/AMERICAN CLOCK.
8-day New Haven movement
with hour strike. Inlaid veneer
case. Ht. 36" 635.00

HANGING GINGERBREAD. Sessions, 8-day with strike and alarm. Oak case, all original. Ht. 28" $395.00

INGRAHAM TIMEPIECE. 8-day. Mission style oak case, all original. Ht. 32¼" $365.00

E.N. WELCH TIMEPIECE. 8-day. Walnut case. Ht. 38" $425.00

NEW HAVEN WALL CLOCK. 8-day, ½-hour strike. Walnut case. Ht. 18" $395.00

ENGLISH CLOCKS

Left to Right —
ENGLISH TAVERN CLOCK. By Samuel Buxton, Norfolk.
8-day, time only. Oak case restored. Ca. 1770. Ht. 60" $2500.00
ENGLISH TAVERN CLOCK. By Abbott, London. 8-day,
time only. Oak case. Ca. 1795. Ht. 40" 2800.00
LONGCASE WALL CLOCK. By J. Whitaker, Guisbro, England.
8-day, time only. Oak case. Early 1800's. Ht. 57" 2500.00

> TAVERN CLOCK: Name for a style of clock with a large dial displayed in a
> prominent position in taverns and inns in the 18th century.
> Often referred to as Act of Parliament Clocks, the 1897 tax on clocs in
> England and increasing coaching facilities made this type of clock popular.

SKELTON CLOCK: Clocks with an exposed movement with the plate cut away or pierced to show the action of the movement, usually covered with a glass dome.

Note: Domes removed to photograph.

Above — Left —
SKELTON CLOCK. In the shape of Canterbury Cathedral. By Smiths, London. 8-day, two train fusee. Hour strike on gong, ½-hour strike on bell. Ca. 1860.
Ht. 19" $2250.00

Above — Right —
SKELTON CLOCK. English, 8-day, fusee movement with passing hour strike. Silvered dial, white marble base. Ca. 1850.
Ht. 15" 1800.00

Left —
SKELTON CLOCK. English, 8-day, time only. Scroll frame stands on red velvet pad over wood base. Ca. 1865. Ht. 10" . . 975.00

Above — Left —
ENGLISH mahogany bracket clock
by Payne, New Bond St., London.
8-day two train fusee movement,
half deadbeat escapement, ¼-hour
strike on two bells. Ca. 1840.
Ht. 24" $3600.00

Above — Right —
ENGLISH bracket clock. By William
Grant, London. 8-day, strike on bell.
Double fusee verge escapement, bob
pendulum. Engraved back plate.
Dark walnut veneer case. Ca. 1760.
Ht. 16½" 2950.00

Left —
ENGLISH 3 train fusee, 8-day,
quarter chiming on 9 gongs.
Choice of St. Michaels or West-
minster chimes. Silver dial.
Ca. 1900.
Ht. 16½" 1200.00

ENGLISH four glass mantel timepiece by James McCabe. 8-day balance movement with fusee. Serial no. 2354, Ca. 1835. Hand carved ebony veneer case. Ht. 8" $2500.00

QUEEN ANNE PERIOD. English 30-hour with single hand and hour strike. Bird cage movement. Oak case, Ca. 1700. . . $3800.00

Above —
ENGLISH DIAL CLOCK. 8-day, fusee and chain. Mahogany frame. Diam. 12" $455.00

Left —
ENGLISH FUSEE WALL CLOCK. 8-day, double fusee, time and strike. On dial "John Hall & Co., Manchester." Oak case, Ca. 1855. Ht. 24½" 550.00

PUNCH CLOCK.
By National Time Recorder
Co., London.
Ht. 35" $550.00

MINIATURE REPRODUCTION
OF ENGLISH LANTERN CLOCK.
By Smiths English Clocks Ltd.
Brass case, 7 jewel, 8-day movement.
Ca. 1950. Ht. 7" $165.00

NOTE:

From the earliest days of clock making in Britain it was the custom to produce clocks exclusively for the wealthy.

In the late 1800's foreigners took advantage of this situation and millions of inexpensive clocks from Germany and the United States were imported to fill the need of the man in the street. These are often found with the names of British jewellers on the dial.

STIRRUP FRAME CLOCK. By
Smiths, England. 8-day, white
luminous dial and hands.
Suspended on leather. Ht. 6"
Dial diam. 2¼" $95.00

69

FRENCH CLOCKS

Above — Left —
FRENCH EMPIRE MANTEL CLOCK.
14-day, ½-hour strike. White marble
pillars, base and top. Gilded cupids,
ornaments and pineapple finials.
Sunray pendulum, porcelain dial
decorated with roses. 1860/70.
Ht. 21" $1400.00

Above — Right —
FRENCH 8-DAY CLOCK.
With tic-tac movement.
Ormulu and cobalt blue
enamel case.
Ht. 12" 1200.00

Left —
FRENCH 15-DAY CLOCK.
Hour and ½-hour strike movement.
Cloisonne case marked "Tiffany."
Floral decoration on blue ground,
gilded brass frame. Enamel dial
with garlands of roses.
Ht. 9½" 2500.00

Above — Left —
SEVRES PORCELAIN CLOCK.
8-day with ½-hour strike. Blue
with 22K hand tooled decoration.
Ht. 12½" $1295.00

Above — Right —
FRENCH 14-DAY TIMEPIECE.
Pendulum movement with silk
suspension. Gilded case with
man playing musical instrument.
Ca. 1820. Ht. 10" . . 850.00

Left —
FRENCH 14-DAY CLOCK.
Gilded case. Green elephant
marked "Luneville" (Limoges).
Ca. 1880. Ht. 15" . . 1500.00

Above — Left —
FRENCH MARBLE CLOCK.
14-day with ½-hour strike.
Spelter figure, brass trim.
Ht. 18½" $525.00

Above — Right —
FRENCH MARBLE CLOCK.
By Japy, Paris. 14-day with
½-hour strike. Brass mounts.
Ca. 1880.
Ht. 17½" 450.00

Left —
BOULLE TIMEPIECE.
Louis XVI style, 8-day balance
movement, time only.
Ca. 1915. . . . . 595.00

FRENCH ORMULU CLOCK.
14-day with ½-hour strike.
Ca. 1885.
Ht. 15½" $650.00

FRENCH 14-DAY CLOCK.
With ½-hour strike. Spelter case
with alabaster inserts. Ca. 1885.
Ht. 14" $350.00

FRENCH ALABASTER CLOCK.
Japy Freres movement. 14-day,
hour and ½-hour strike. Ca. 1848.
Ht. 15½" $375.00

FRENCH 14-DAY TIMEPIECE.
Spelter case, Ca. 1870.
Ht. 12" $275.00

FRENCH BOULLE. Late Empire. By LeRoy, Paris. 14-day, ½-hour strike. Silk suspension. Case inlaid with brass, ivory and tortoise shell.
Ht. 12" $1450.00

FRENCH BRACKET CLOCK. In English style. 14-day, ¼-hour chime on two gongs. Regulator and chime/silent dials. Ca. 1880.
Ht. 15" $795.00

Above —
FRENCH BRACKET CLOCK. In the English style. 14-day, ¼-hour strike on 2 gongs. Mahogany veneer case.
Ca. 1870. Ht. 18" $685.00
Left —
FRENCH LOUIS XVI STYLE. 8-day timepiece. Tortoise shell case with ormulu mounts. Ca. 1890.
Ht. handle up. 10" 875.00

CRYSTAL REGULATOR: Similar to the crystal clock, but with superior movement and mercury compensated pendulum.

Above — Left —
CRYSTAL REGULATOR.
French, 14-day, ½-hour strike, mercury pendulum. Oval case, bevelled glasses.
Marked "Tiffany" on porcelain dial. Late 1800's.
Ht. 12" $995.00

Above — Right —
CRYSTAL REGULATOR.
French, 15-day movement.
Ca. 1890.
Ht. 10½" 695.00

Left —
FRENCH "CRYSTAL" CLOCK.
14-day, strike on bell, visible escapement. Exceptionally large for this type of clock.
Ht. 14" 795.00

CRYSTAL CLOCK: A North American name for table or mantel clocks with glass cases framed in brass.

75

FRENCH MARBLE CLOCK. With Westminster chime. 8-day, two barrel, chime and strike, five gongs. Brass decorative accessories. Ht. 19½" $1200.00

FRENCH MARBLE CLOCK. Black with pink. 14-day, ½-hour strike. Enamel dial. Ca. 1890. Ht. 10¼" $295.00

FRENCH MARBLE CLOCK. Black with coloured marble inserts. 14-day, ½-hour strike, porcelain dial. Ca. 1880. Ht. 12¾" $230.00

FRENCH MARBLE TIMEPIECE. Black and green. 14-day, time only movement. Porcelain dial. Ca. 1905. Ht. 10" $155.00

FRENCH FRAME CLOCK.
8-day with double strike (it strikes
at the hour and again two minutes
after) also strikes ½-hours. Black
frame with mother-of-pearl inserts.
White porcelain dial. Made in Jura
area of France.
Ht 24½" $695.00

Above —
MORBIER CLOCK. 8-day with
double strike, also strikes ½-hours.
Repousse brass case and pendulum.
Brass hands, porcelain dial. Made
in Jura area of France, Ca. 1882.
All original. Ht. 56"
Diam. of dial 8½" . . $1250.00

Left —
GILDED FRAME CLOCK. 8-day
French movement. Grande
Sonnerie strike and music box.
Pull repeat and pull for music
box. Porcelain dial.
Ht. 21½" 695.00

Left — FRENCH 8-DAY CLOCK.
Hour and ½-hour strike, silk suspension. Rosewood case with moulded
bakelite pseudo carving. Porcelain
dial marked "Henry Mark" —
not maker. Ht. 9¾" $575.00

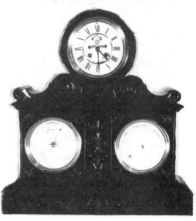

Above —
FRENCH 14-DAY CLOCK.
½-hour strike, visible escapement. Black marble case,
barometer and thermometer
in lower section.
Ht. 18½" $750.00

Above —
FRENCH BAROMETER & CLOCK.
8-day clock with ½-hour strike. Heavy
brass cases. Ht. 27"
Pair $2200.00
Right —
FRENCH 8-DAY TIMEPIECE.
With jewelled lever escapement.
Hand carved English case with
barometer and thermometer in
lower section. Ca. 1885.
Ht. 19" 450.00

GERMAN CLOCKS

Above —
SYMPHONION DISC MUSIC
BOX/CLOCK.
Walnut case.
German, Ca. 1900.
30-hour clock, disc music
box played at the hour or
as an alarm.
Ht. 12" $1800.00

Left —
GERMAN BRACKET OR
MANTEL CLOCK.
8-day crown wheel escapement
with strike. Mock pendulum
behing aperture in dial.
Clocks of this type were called
Chimney clocks in Germany.
Ht. 20" 800.00

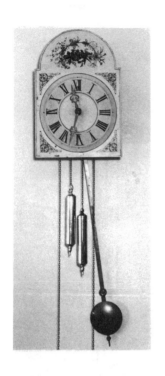

Above — Left —
GERMAN WAG-ON-THE-WALL.
30-hour with strike, brass plates.
Iron case, metal dial.
Ca. 1840.
Dial Ht. 18" $795.00

Above — Right —
GERMAN WAG-ON-THE-WALL.
Postman's alarm, 30-hour. White
porcelain dial with pink chapter
ring. Ca. 1870.
Case Diam. 10½" 495.00

Left —
GERMAN FRAME CLOCK.
30-hour, ½-hour strike, brass
pendulum, weights and chain.
Porcelain dial with gilded
repousse surround.
Case Width 11¾" 375.00

Above — Left —
GERMAN WALL CLOCK.
8-day with hour and ½-hour
strike, spring wound. Oak
case, applied carving.
Ca. 1885.
Ht. 32" $525.00

Above — Right —
GERMAN WALL CLOCK.
8-day, ½-hour strike.
Walnut case. Ca. 1895.
Ht. 52" 680.00

Left —
GERMAN 8-DAY WALL CLOCK.
Strikes hours and ½-hours on
gong, brass pendulum bob.
Walnut case.
Ht. 21" 235.00

Above — Left —
GERMAN BRACKET CLOCK.
By Winterhalder & Hofmeier.
8-day with ting-tang ¼-hour
chime. Ca. 1895.
Ht. 20" $975.00

Above — Right —
GERMAN 8-DAY CLOCK.
¼-hour ting-tang strike movement. English carved oak case,
solid brass mounts and finial,
silvered chapter ring.
Ca. 1890.
Ht. 19¼" 895.00

Left —
GERMAN BRACKET CLOCK.
By Kienzle. 8-day with West-
minster chime. Walnut case.
Ca. 1930. Ht. 17" . . 550.00

JUNGHAMS WESTMINSTER CHIME
CLOCK. 8-day, chime and strike.
Mahogany veneer inlaid case.
Ht. 17¼" $500.00

MINIATURE JUNGHAMS TIME-
PIECE. 8-day, time only, oak case.
Ca. 1890's. Ht. 13" . . . $350.00

JUNGHAMS CHIME CLOCK.
8-day, chime on rods. Silvered
dial. Ht. 15" $495.00

JUNGHAMS WESTMINSTER CHIME
CLOCK. 8-day with chime/silent and
regulator dials. Art deco mahogany
case. 1930's. Ht. 13" $585.00

JUNGHAMS 30-HOUR BALANCE
WHEEL CLOCK. Molded oak case.
Ca. 1910. Ht. 7½" $135.00

GERMAN 8-DAY TIMEPIECE.
Oak case. Ca. 1925.
Ht. 14½" $225.00

GERMAN MANTEL CLOCK.
8-day pendulum movement, hour
and ½-hour strike. Walnut case.
Ht. 17" $225.00

GERMAN WESTMINSTER CHIME
CLOCK. By Haller, Wurtemburg.
8-day two barrel pendulum movement. Oak case. Ht. 14" $350.00

Left —
GERMAN 8-DAY MANTEL
CLOCK. Pendulum movement,
½-hour strike, engraved silver
dial.
Sitzendorf porcelain case.
1870's.
Ht. 12" $2200.00

AUSTRIAN TEMPLE CLOCK.
30-hour with verge escapement,
Grande Sonnerie striking and
calendar. Fusee in gone train
only, pull repeat. Hand painted
porcelain plaques on case.
Ca. 1765.
Ht. 25" $3900.00

AUSTRIAN WALL CLOCK.
8-day pendulum movement
with hour strike, silk suspension, solid brass plates. Signed
hand painted dial mount with
antelopes and peacocks in a
garden. Ca. 1860.
Ht. 26" $1800.00

VIENNA REGULATOR: A wall clock made in Austria or Germany. Weight driven with deadbeat escapement, the pendulum rod is usually made of wood. Vienna Regulators are frequently fitted with seconds hand and dial, however, since the pendulums do not beat full seconds, the hand completes its revolution in less than one minute.

Above — Left —
GUSTAV BECKER REGULATOR. 8-day, hour strike. Walnut veneer case with lions and a horse. Ca. 1875. Ht. 64" $2600.00

Above — Centre —
VIENNA REGULATOR. 8-day, ½-hour strike. Unusual oak case. Ht. 44" 1700.00

Above — Right —
SERPENTINE VIENNA REGULATOR. 8-day, ½-hour strike, brass weights and pendulum, porcelain dial. Walnut case with applied tulip leaf carving. 1860 - 70. Ht. 48" 2400.00

Left —
VIENNA REGULATOR. Time and ½-hour strike. Intricately carved case with double key hole front. Ca. 1880. Ht. 56" 2100.00

Above — Left —
VIENNA REGULATOR. 8-day, ½-hour strike.
Carved walnut case. Ht. 52" $2200.00

Above — Centre —
VIENNA REGULATOR. 8-day, time only.
Ht. 40" 1200.00

Above — Right —
VIENNA REGULATOR. 8-day, spring wound,
time and strike. All original.
Ca. 1890. Ht. 48" 675.00

Left —
VIENNA REGULATOR. 8-day, spring wound,
strike on gong. New horse.
Ca. 1890. Ht. 35" 495.00

GRANDFATHER CLOCKS

Left to Right —

TWISS GRANDFATHER CLOCK. 30-hour wood works, original tin can weights. "J.B. & R. Twiss" on restored dial. Pine case. Ca. 1820. Ht. 6' $4600.00

GRANDFATHER CLOCK. English movement, 8-day with strike. "James G. Hanna, Quebec" on dial. Unusual brass crown hands. Mahogany veneer pine case. Ht. 7' 4" 5500.00

GRANDFATHER CLOCK. By unknown English maker. 8-day, hour strike on bell. Oak case inlaid with mahogany. Painted break-arch dial with rural scenes. Ca. 1820. Ht. 7' 1" 4200.00

SCOTTISH GRANDFATHER CLOCK. By Andrew Dickie. 8-day with hour strike. Brass dial, oyster veneer case. Ca. 1740. Ht. 8' 2" 6250.00

Left to Right —

GRANDFATHER CLOCK. By R. Peacock, Lincoln, England. 8-day,
hour strike on bell. Inlaid mahogany case, rocking ship in coastal
scene. Painted break-arch dial. Ca. 1825. Ht. 7' 2" $4600.00

GRANDFATHER CLOCK. English, 8-day brass works, strike hours
on bell. Unusual brass acorn hands. "Kennedy" on dial.
Ca. 1835. Ht. 6' 11" 3995.00

GRANDFATHER CLOCK. By John Kiddie-Markwich. 8-day with
strike, calendar and second hand. Mahogany case. Painted dial with
scene of "Lady of the Lake" at top, rural scenes and winter scene
round dial. Ca. 1820. Ht. 6' 8" 4250.00

GRANDFATHER CLOCK. English by Thomas Watson, Newcastle.
8-day, hour strike. Oak case, refinished, small repair to case.
Ca. 1790 - 1810. . . . . 3750.00

Left to Right —
GRANDFATHER CLOCK. Scottish, maker not known. 8-day
strike on bell. Walnut veneer, pedestal base. Dial not original.
Ht. 6' 5" $4750.00
GRANDFATHER CLOCK. By Winterhalder & Hofmeier.
Four different chimes. Walnut case. Ca. 1910. Ht. 6' 6" .. 7500.00
GRANDMOTHER CLOCK. English by Charles Vaughan. 30-
hour single weight, strike on bell. Brass dial, oak case.
Ca. 1730. Ht. 6' 2" 3500.00
GRANDMOTHER CLOCK. English 8-day movement, weight
driven time and hour strike. Rosewood and walnut case.
Early 1800's. Ht. 5' 10" 5000.00

HISTORY
of
LONG CASE CLOCKS

The Grandfather's clock was not known by this name until after 1876 when a song "My Grandfather's Clock" became popular. Previously the descriptive name had been Long Case clock. First made about the early 1600's, these clocks were very handsome, and left nothing to be desired in design and workmanship. The "Clock Makers Company" of that time was a tremendous force, and since cost was not important it was possible for the craftsman of the day to produce clocks of a quality in which they could take pride. Any man who did not turn out work of a consistent high standard found that the Guild would confiscate and destroy clocks they considered below standard. If this should happen to a craftsman he might as well close up shop, as his reputation was completely ruined.

Clocks were only available to the truly wealthy in the early stages, and the finest material was used in the making. With the demand for clocks by those of lower incomes, and the loss of power by the great Guild, standards dropped and it is of interest to note the variations of quality of the clocks made for the prosperous and the less prosperous.

Grandfather clocks are usually 6'6" and up, taller than the Grandmother, which is 5'6" to 6' and sometimes shorter. If less than 4'6" the clock is then considered to be a Grand-daughter. These are fairly late innovations and not in the antique category.

The earliest Long Case type were narrow, the dials were square, and not more than 9" or 10" across. Dial centres were often engraved with the lily pattern, which was then a craze of the day. The corner ornaments were beautifully finished, with a great simplicity of style. The hand (there was only one at this time) was a double loop, and often had a bevelled surface. The earliest type of hood had to be taken off or raised before the hand could be touched. Moulding under the hood was convex, as was the moulding at the top of the plynth.

The hood of the case would have twisted pillars, and the movement was of the Lantern type. Ornamentation, if any, consisted of a small quantity of inlay. The door was a narrow rectangular, less in height than in later years.

In 1690 the eight day movement was developed, minute hands and calendar circles became usual, and the cases became more ornamental. Faces with frosted dials were introduced, and became standard on most London-made clocks for about 75 years.

From 1690 to 1790 calendars on clocks were considered to be highly important, even more important than the minute hand. Very few types except Lantern Clocks were made without the calendar. This does not seem strange when one remembers there were no calendars published in those days, or newspapers and radio to keep track of the date.

On clocks of this period the minutes were marked around the outer dial ring, and were quite large, sometimes clockmakers fashioned the minute numeral the same size as the hour figure. Corner ornament styling became fancier and the hour hand began to be a work of art, a fine craftsman would take joy in developing beautiful and intricate designs. The dials became somewhat larger and by 1730 many changes had taken place. The hoods underwent various phases, and some followed the now popular style of arching quite closely while others had amazingly fancy tops, with a very top heavy appearance. It wasn't long before the arched area about the dial became a matter of some comment, and some developed automata, such as swinging Father time or a ship in full sail, others had a moon that would wax and wain. A period of general degeneration of tasteful design took place.

In the towns outside London clockmaking was becoming a major industry and first class workmanship was common in areas away from London, long after the London makers had stopped using the classical and tasteful designs.

There were periods of style, therefore, which overlapped as some originated in London, and were used later in the country districts.

These periods can be defined as the Ebony and Walnut period, Lacquer period and the Mahogany period. During the Lacquer period, the first clocks of this period were done in China, with London makers sending cases there to be lacquered, but the artist in London soon became quite good at copying the technique, and later lacquered English clocks are quite good, and approximate the originals. The ones tried by Provincial craftsmen were indifferent, and few of these are found today.

Much more interest is being shown in the Grandfather clock lately and many are being introduced into Canada by importers. American clockmakers made Long Case clocks from approximately the start of the 1700's and Abel Cottey made clocks in Philadelphia in 1682.

Canadian makers of Grandfather clocks include the Twiss brothers of Montreal, John Geddie, Nova Scotia and John McCulloch of Halifax. There are many others.

Prices of antique Grandfather clocks have risen dramatically in the last few years. There is every indication that prices of good examples, especially those of historical interest to Canadians, will continue their upward trend.

CARRIAGE CLOCKS

Carriage clocks are good quality travel clocks: a development from the 17th and 18th centuries.

The majority of carriage clocks found today are of French origin, however, they were also made in several other countries including England, Germany and America.

They range from simple timepieces to clocks with alarm and/or strike to complicated models with calendars and complex strike mechanisms. Many of the more expensive models were housed in elaborate cases. Customarily a velvet lined carrying case, usually leather, was supplied, but many of these have been lost or discarded.

In recent years these clocks have become a popular collectable and are also in vogue as domestic clocks.

CARRIAGE CLOCK. By Charles Frodsham, London, England. Lever escapement, strike with repeat and alarm. Ca. 1950' Ht. 7¼" $2000.00

FRENCH CARRIAGE CLOCK. 8-day, strike and alarm with repeat, jewelled lever platform escapement. Late 1800's. Ht. 7¼" $1500.00

FRENCH CARRIAGE CLOCK. 8-day with alarm, jewelled lever platform escapement. Bevelled glass. Ht. 6¼" $950.00

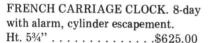

FRENCH CARRIAGE CLOCK. 8-day
with alarm, cylinder escapement.
Ht. 5¾" $625.00

FRENCH CARRIAGE CLOCK.
8-day with alarm, lever escapement.
Ht. 6" $950.00

FRENCH CARRIAGE CLOCK. 8-day,
time only, cylinder escapement.
Ht. 5¼" $595.00

FRENCH CARRIAGE CLOCK. 8-day
jewelled lever platform escapement.
Sold by Henry Birks & Sons Ltd.
Ht. 5¾" $895.00

FRENCH CARRIAGE CLOCKS. 8-day. Left to Right —
Time and alarm, cylinder movement, porcelain dials. Ht. 6" . . $ 795.00
Time and strike with repeat, plus alarm. Lever movement.
All over richly engraved case made for the Chinese market.
Ht. 7" 2000.00
Time and strike with hour repeat, lever movement, porcelain
dial marked "Ryrie Bros., Toronto." Ht. 5½" 985.00

FRENCH CARRIAGE CLOCKS. 8-day. Left to Right —
Time only, jewelled lever, platform escapement. Porcelain
dial. Ht. 6" . . . . $ 790.00
Time only, cylinder escapement, front set with brilliants,
filligree frame round porcelain dial. Ht. 6"
With leather case, not shown. 800.00
Time and alarm, cylinder escapement, porcelain dials. Ht. 6" . . 750.00

FRENCH CARRIAGE CLOCK. 8-day, time and alarm, jewelled lever platform escapement. Green enamel dials, cloisonne borders. Late 1800's. Ht. 6¼" $1200.00

CARRIAGE CLOCK. Swiss jewelled lever platform movement. Art Nouveau sterling silver case. Ht. 3½" $545.00

NEW HAVEN CARRIAGE CLOCK. 8-day, ½-hour strike and repeat. Gilt case, bevelled glass. 1890's. Ht. 6" $650.00

WATERBURY CARRIAGE CLOCK. Meteor model, Ca. 1908. 30-hour strike with repeat. Brass case. $450.00

SHIPS' CLOCKS

The custom of sounding ship's bells to mark the passing of time was established at least as early as the 15th century.

Each 24 hours was divided into four hour periods of duty known as "watches." Shortened watches known as "dog-watches" allowed for the evening meal.

Generally ship's bell clocks take no account of "dog-watches," and ring the half-hours and hours as per schedule below. The bell is rung in pairs with a pause between each pair.

8-DAY SHIP'S BELL CLOCK.
By Seth Thomas. Nickel plated case.
Diam. 7" $300.00

CHELSEA CLOCK CO., Boston, Mass. Miniature ship's clock. Cast brass case. $325.00

8 p.m.	—	12 a.m.	— First watch
12 a.m.	—	4 a.m.	— Middle watch
4 a.m.	—	8 a.m.	— Morning watch
8 a.m.	—	12 p.m.	— Forenoon watch
12 p.m.	—	4 p.m.	— Afternoon watch
4 p.m.	—	6 p.m.	— First dog watch
6 p.m.	—	8 p.m.	— Last dog watch

a.m.	p.m.		
12.30	12.30	1 bell	●
1.00	1.00	2 bells	●●
1.30	1.30	3 „	●● ●
2.00	2.00	4 „	●● ●●
2.30	2.30	5 „	●● ●● ●
3.00	3.00	6 „	●● ●● ●●
3.30	3.30	7 „	●● ●● ●● ●
4.00	4.00	8 „	●● ●● ●● ●●
4.30	4.30	1 „	●
5.00	5.00	2 „	●●
5.30	5.30	3 „	●● ●
6.00	6.00	4 „	●● ●●
6.30	6.30	5 „	●● ●● ●
7.00	7.00	6 „	●● ●● ●●
7.30	7.30	7 „	●● ●● ●● ●
8.00	8.00	8 „	●● ●● ●● ●●
8.30	8.30	1 „	●
9.00	9.00	2 „	●●
9.30	9.30	3 „	●● ●
10.00	10.00	4 „	●● ●●
10.30	10.30	5 „	●● ●● ●
11.00	11.00	6 „	●● ●● ●●
11.30	11.30	7 „	●● ●● ●● ●
12.00	12.00	8 „	●● ●● ●● ●●

FRENCH SHIP'S CLOCK. 8-day cylinder movement, brass case. Diam. 7" $195.00

Left —
SHIP'S CLOCK.
8-day, jewelled lever platform
escapement movement in brass
case.
On dial "Kelvin, Bottomley and
Baird, Glasgow & London."
Ca. 1914   . . . .$300.00

Right —
SHIP'S BOILER ROOM CLOCK.
8-day by Seth Thomas.
In black composition case.
Diam. 7¾" $295.00

Left —
ENGLISH SHIP'S TIMEPIECE.
8-day in brass case.
Diam. 7½" $250.00

Right —
ENGLISH SHIP'S CLOCK.
Lever escapement movement
with fusee and chain.
Ca. 1900. Legs fitted later.
Diam. 6" $525.00

SHIP'S CHRONOMETERS

An extremely accurate timepiece in a box, suspended in gimbal rings in order to remain level when a ship rolls and pitches. An accurate clock or watch is necessary for navigation, since it is essential to know the exact time to find the longitudinal position of a ship at sea. All large vessels carry one of these fine instruments.

SHIP'S CHRONOMETER.
By John Bruce & Sons,
Liverpool, England.
Early 1900's. . . $2500.00

Above —
SHIP'S CHRONOMETER. By Thomas Mercer, St. Albans, England.
No 23002, 2-day movement with up/down indicator. Complete with box and outer case.
1940/50. . . . . $1500.00

Left —
SHIP'S CHRONOMETER. By Ulysse Nardin, Le Locle, Switzerland.
Chronometer escapement and helical hairspring. Complete with box, gimbal rings and outer case.
Dial diam. 3¾" 3000.00

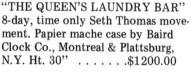

"THE QUEEN'S LAUNDRY BAR"
8-day, time only Seth Thomas movement. Papier mache case by Baird
Clock Co., Montreal & Plattsburg,
N.Y. Ht. 30" $1200.00

"THE SNOWDRIFT BAKING
POWDER CO., Brantford, Ont."
8-day, time only Seth Thomas
movement. Papier mache case
by Baird Clock Co.
Bezel missing.
Ht. 30" $800.00

Left —
"MILKMAID MILK"
8-day, time only. British
Empire Clock Co. movement.
Embossed metal frame on wood
case by Baird Clock Co.
Diam. 17" $550.00

Right —
"L.O. GROTHE &
CO., Montreal."
"The Boston
Cigar"
"The Peg Top
Cigar"
Clock frame by Acme
Litho Co., Ansonia
clock not original.
Ht. 11½" $450.00

Left —
"ST. CHARLES
EVAPORATED
CREAM"
Cast iron cow with
brass finish.
30-hour movement
by The Westclox
Manufacturing Co.,
LaSalle, Ill.
Ht. 8½" . . $300.00

Right —
"GILLETT'S GOODS ARE THE
BEST"
"E.W. Gillett, London, Chicago,
Toronto"
Bronzed cast iron frame. Alarm
clock movement by Westclox,
not original.
Diam. 11½" $550.00

"EVER-READY SAFETY RAZOR"
8-day, time only, two mainspring
balance wheel movement.
Litho tin case.
Ht. 17½" $2500.00

STORE REGULATOR. "Delicious,
Drink Coca-Cola" on dial. By the
E. Ingraham Clock Co., Bristol, Conn.
1905 - 07. 8-day, time only. Refinished
oak case. 17½" x 38½" . . . $2000.00

ELECTRIC CLOCK. Internally lit
with two bulbs. Reverse painted
on glass. 1960's.
15¼" x 15¼" $150.00

ELECTRIC CLOCK. Enamelled
tin, red centre, brown surround
with gold numerals. American.
1961. Diam. 17" $90.00

ALARM CLOCKS

WESTCLOCK BABY BEN. 30-hour with alarm. Black dial with luminous hands and numerals. Ca. 1930.
Dial diam. 2¼" $55.00

WESTCLOX BABY BEN. 30-hour, "repeat" and "steady" alarm. Pink case, gold numerals on white paper dial. Ca. 1930.
Dial diam. 2¼" $60.00

WESTCLOX SILVER BELL. 30-hour with alarm. Ca. 1905 - 1910.
Dial diam. 4" $75.00

BELL ALARM CLOCK. By Chicago Clock Co. Unusual 30-hour clock with dial illustrating famous British personalities, including Queen Victoria, and Royal Coat of Arms. Late 1800's.
Ht. 5" $175.00

WESTCLOX BIG BEN ALARM CLOCKS. All with repeat.
Value .... $60.00 - $80.00

Left — WESTCLOX BABY BEN. 1930's. $55.00
Centre — WESTCLOX BEN HUR. 1930's............... 75.00
Right — ANSONIA CLOCK CO. On dial "W.W. Crue,
Watchmaker & Jeweller, Summerside, P.E.I." 65.00

WESTCLOX BIG BEN. Similar movements in both. Early 1920's.
Left — Made in Peterborough, Ontario. Ht. handle up 7" $95.00
Right — Made in LaSalle, Ill. Ht. 6" 85.00

NICKEL PLATED ALARM CLOCKS
Above — Left to Right —
Dawn of Day, Wurtemburg, Germany. Ca. 1910.
Ht. 6½" $50.00
Columbia 8-day alarm, Sessions Clock Co.
Pat'd. Dec. 1912. Ht. 7" 55.00
German 30-hour alarm. Ca. 1920. Ht. 6¼" 40.00
Left —
Bayard 30-hour French alarm clock.
Sonnfor model. Luminous hands and
numerals. Dial diam. 5" 50.00
Below — Left —
Junghams bell alarm. German, 30-hour.
Nickel plated, silvered dial. Ca. 1905.
Dial diam. 1¾" 35.00
Below — Right —
Small bell alarm. 30-hour. Wasp model.
On dial "F.G. England, Regina, Sask."
Ht. 3¾" 60.00

30-HOUR ALARM. In brass case with "Junior Tatoo Movement." Pat'd. 1904 . . . . $60.00

TOM-TOM True Time Teller by New Haven Clock Co. 30-hour alarm. Ht. 5" $50.00

Above — Left —
TIME KING ALARM. Made in Bristol, Conn. Nickel plated brass case. 4½" square $35.00

Above — Right —
NEW HAVEN ALARM CLOCK. 30-hour. White metal case. Ht. 5½" 90.00

Left —
NEW HAVEN 'ART LARM' 8-day in brown bakelite case. Ht. 5¼" 35.00

GERMAN TRAVEL CLOCK. 30-hour with alarm. Nickel plated brass case. Ht. handle up 5¼" $75.00

GERMAN ALARM. 30-hour with music box. Nickel plated, polished to brass case. Trade mark — half moon with B. Ca. 1890. Ht. 7" $175.00

GERMAN 30-HOUR ALARM. Nickel plated case. Ca. 1910. Ht. handle up 7¼" . . $100.00

AMERICAN 30-HOUR ALARM. By Gilbert Clock Co., Winstead, Conn. Pat'd. July, 1885. Nickel plated case. Ht. 8½" $185.00

GERMAN TWO BELL ALARM.
30-hour, winds from back.
Ht. 11" $125.00

GERMAN TWO BELL ALARM.
30-hour with lever alarm stop.
Wood case, complete except for
fret at top. Ca. 1890.
Ht. 9" $135.00

COTTAGE CLOCK. 30-hour with alarm.
All original.
Label — "Teutonia Clock Manufactory."
German copy of American 30-hour alarm
clock.
Ht. 9" $125.00

30-HOUR ALARM. American.
Iron case with mother-of pearl
inlay. Ht. 9" $95.00

30-HOUR DRUM OR TIN
CAN ALARM. German.
Velvet box case. Clock can
be removed from case.
Ht. 9¼" $55.00

30-HOUR ALARM. By Seth
Thomas. Cast metal case.
Ca. 1910.
Ht. 9" $85.00

JUNGHAMS 30-HOUR ALARM
CLOCK. Castle shaped case.
Ht. 12" $150.00

Above — Left —
GINGERBREAD ALARM CLOCK. By New
Haven Clock Co. 8-day with strike and alarm.
Oak case. All original. Ca. 1915.
Ht. 22" $260.00

Above — Right —
RENDULUM ALARM CLOCK. 8-day with
patent automatic alarm by Fattorini & Sons,
Bradford, England. Ht. 18" 230.00

Left —
30-HOUR ALARM CLOCK. By Sochard,
U.S.A. Wood case. Ca. 1930.
Ht. 5" 30.00

Right —
30-HOUR ALARM
CLOCK. By New
Haven Clock Co.
On dial "Intermittent."
Wood case. Ca. 1904.
Ht. 5" $35.00

OTHER CLOCKS
OF
INTEREST

BOUDOIR CLOCK. 30-hour
movement, key wind.
Ormulu case marked "Paris"
on base. Early 1900's.
Ht. 4½" $350.00

FIGURAL CLOCK. Young man
carrying bale of cotton. German
balance movement, 8-day with
bim-bam strike on hour and
½-hour. Italian gilded brass case.
Ca. 1950. Ht. 14"
Dial diam. 3½"   . . . $1000.00

SWISS 30-HOUR CLOCK.
Jewelled lever. Bell can be
seen moving in tower when
clock is going. Green marble
case with gilding and black
enamel front. Ca. 1910.
Ht. 2½" $700.00

UPSON BROS. 8-day, hour and
strike. Cast iron case with mother-
of-pearl inlay. Ca. 1855.
Ht. 17" $495.00

OWEN & CLARK. 8-day with
hour strike. Cast iron case with
mother-of-pearl inlay. Case over-
painted, bezel missing. Ca. 1857.
Ht. 20" $150.00

NEW HAVEN. 8-day, ½-hour strike.
Cast iron case, with gilt pillars.
Ca. 1890. Ht. 10¾" $210.00

BLIND PERSON'S CLOCK.
European 8-day with strike on
bell. Jewelled lever movement.
Cast iron case, extra thick hands,
raised numerals, no bezel or
glass. Ht. 8½" $175.00

Right —
FRAME CLOCK.
English frame marked
"Tablot Pewter."
German movement.
Late 1920's.
4½" x 3¾" $55.00

Left —
ART DECO BOUDOIR
CLOCK.
Waterbury 30-hour movement.
Patented 1894.
Ht. 3¼" $55.00

IVORINE NOVELTY CLOCK.
Original French 30-hour movement. Cream coloured bird on
black wood base.
Dial diam. 1¾" $65.00

NOVELTY CLOCK. German,
maker unknown. 30-hour
balance movement. Wood case,
eyes revolve slowly, hands not
original.
Early 1900's. $115.00

MINIATURES

Left — 30-HOUR TRAVEL CLOCK. Psuedo pendulum showing in aperture at bottom of dial. Mother-of-pearl front and base, in leather case. Ca. 1900. Ht. 3" $250.00

Centre — 30-HOUR CARRIAGE CLOCK. Swiss, marked on dial "Mignon." Brass and glass case, celluloid dial. Ht. 3" 275.00

Right — DESK CLOCK. Silver plated case. 18 size E. Howard & Co., Boston watch movement, 30-hour, 15 jewel, No. 45103 with silver dial, wound from other side of post. Ca. 1880. Ht. 4" 400.00

Left — 30-HOUR CLOCK IN BRASS CASE. Pendulum movement, wind and hand change at back with same key. Marked on back "Yale Clock Co., Newhaven, Conn." Pat'd. 1880.
Ht. 3" .... $250.00 - $300.00
Right — THE PARKER & WHIPPLE CO., Meriden, Conn. 30-hour movement. On dial "A.E. Hotchkiss' Patent." All brass case, paper dial. Late 1800's. .... $250.00 - $300.00

JAEGER LE COULTRE PENDANT WATCH. Converts to a travel clock. Wrist watch movement with alarm. Silver with black enamel. 1930's.
Ht. 2" $250.00

BOUDOIR

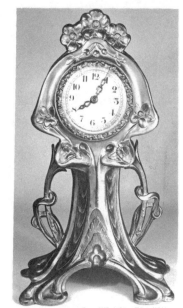

ART NOUVEAU BOUDOIR CLOCK.
30-hour movement, gilt case.
Ca. 1900' Ht. 8½" $200.00

ART NOUVEAU BOUDOIR CLOCK.
8-day timepiece, gilded case.
Ca. 1910. Ht. 12" $160.00

ART NOUVEAU BOUDOIR CLOCK.
By New Haven Clock Co. 30-hour
movement, gilded case. Ht. 9" $175.00

ART NOUVEAU BOUDOIR CLOCK.
German 30-hour movement.
Ht. 9¼" $155.00

BOUDOIR CLOCKS. 30-hour in china cases. Early 1900's.
Ht. of tallest 6" Each $75.00

30-HOUR GERMAN MOVEMENT.
In bisque imitation Wedgwood case,
white on green ground. Celluloid
and brass dial, gilded brass bezel.
Ht. 7" $85.00

30-HOUR NEW HAVEN MOVE-
MENT. Patent applied for 1904.
Blue on white china case, marked
"Foreign." Ht. 9" $75.00

BULLE ELECTRIC CLOCK.
Magnetic impulse, battery
driven. Glass dome removed
for photo.
Ht. 9¾" $595.00

POOLE ELECTRIC BATTERY
CLOCK. Made by the Morse
Chain Co., Ithica, N.Y. Spirit
level in base. Black stand, gilt
bezel and silvered dial. Gilt
pendulum. Ht. 8½" Diam. of
base 7½" Glass dome removed
for photo. $225.00

ATMOS CLOCK. A Swiss clock made by Jaeger-Le-Coultre,
wound by changes in temperature and atmospheric pressure.
With original box and packing. Ca. 1940. . . . . . .$1200.00

LUX CLOCKS

Formed by Paul Lux in 1917 the Lux Clock Company of Waterbury, Connecticut and Lebanon, Tennessee made small novelty clocks, timers and alarms.

Their animated pendulettes and other small clocks are popular with collectors.

LUX CLOCKS.
30-hour,
working pendulums,
false weights.
Left —
BLUEBIRD
Ht. 5" $75.00
Right —
BLUEBIRD
DOVE STYLE.
Ht. 4¼" 75.00

LUX CLOCK. 30-hour, gilded case and velvet hanger.
Ht. with hanger 14" . . $125.00

LUX CLOCK. Dr. Jekyll.
30-hour, composition figure.
Ht. 6½" $150.00

SWINGERS

The swinging clocks illustrated here are from the late 19th century and typical of those that may be found today.

The largest manufacturer of swingers was Junghams of Germany, also many were made in the United States.

These 8-day clocks, although not very good timekeepers, are scarce and bring good prices.

Right —
JUNGHAMS 8-day swinging clock.
Ht. 13½" $1200.00

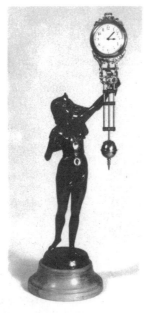

JUNGHAMS 8-day swinging clock.
Base refinished.
Ht. 17½" $1200.00

ANSONIA SWINGER."Huntress"
8-day ball movement. Ca. 1880.
Ht. 25" $2000.00

Above — Left —
CHINESE TABLE OR MANTEL CLOCK.
8-day, hour strike, double fusee and
crown wheel escapement. Seconds hand
does not register seconds, pendulum is
80 beat. Porcelain dial. Three part case,
mixed woods mainly teak, mother-of-
pearl inlay. Main body of clock swivels
on base for winding. Back plate engraved
in Chinese style. Ht. 18" . . $3000.00

Above — Right —
MINIATURE CHINESE TABLE CLOCK.
14-day, hour strike. Engraved verge and
pendulum, double fusee movement,
sweep seconds hand, porcelain dial.
Elaborately carved rosewood case with
mother-of-pearl inlay.
Ca. 1810. Ht. 10" 2500.00

Left —
LARGE CHINESE TABLE CLOCK.
14-day, hour strike. Engraved verge,
double fusee movement. Carved rosewood case, porcelain dial surrounded by
engraved gilded brass plate. Ca. 1810.
Ht. 20" 2200.00

120

GLOSSARY

ALABASTER: a translucent, whitish, fine-grained variety of gypsum.

ARBOR: shafts, axles or spindles of a clock.

BALANCE WHEEL: an oscillating wheel with a hairspring that regulates the escape of power and is the timekeeping element.

BALL OR BUN FOOT: round flattened foot.

BARREL: cylindrical box, usually brass, which contains a mainspring.

BEAT: tick of a clock. A clock is said to be "in beat" when the tick is even.

BEZEL: metal frame that holds glass in place over the clock dial.

BIM-BAM: strike where two different notes are sounded.

BIRD CAGE MOVEMENT: a clock movement in the bottom of a bird cage or a spring driven brass clock of early to mid seventeenth century.

BOB: weight at end of pendulum.

BOB PENDULUM: short pendulum used with verge or tic-tac escapement.

BOMBE: French, "blown out." A bulbous design.

BOOK WEIGHT: weight in the shape of a book to conform to the style of a clock case.

BOULLE OR BUHL: a type of ornamentation using tortoise shell as a base with decorative inlays, either brass, ivory or silver. One of the greatest masters of this type of work was Andre Charles Boulle (1642-1732). He did not invent the process, but such was his skill that it became known by his name.

BRACKET: clock shelf supported by brackets.

BRACKET CLOCK: clock designed to stand on a bracket or shelf.

CHAPTER RING: the ring on the clock dial on which the hours and minutes are engraved or painted.

CHIMNEY CLOCK: European name for mantel clock.

COMPENSATION PENDULUM: the distance between the centre of gravity of the pendulum and its anchorage remains constant at varying temperatures. The two principal forms are the Harrison pendulum and the Graham mercurial pendulum.

COTTAGE CLOCK: a small clock from the latter half of the 19th century. Spring wound, 30-hour, occasionally 8-day, with or without alarm, usually in a wood case.

DIAL CLOCK: a round clock and case, sometimes referred to as a kitchen or office dial.

ESCAPEMENT: the heart of every timepiece of mechanical nature; the device by which the escape of power is regulated. Three types of escapement are: the dead beat, the detached and the recoil.

FUSEE: a "gear changer" as the mainspring runs down, it preserves more or less constant torque on the train as long as the clock is going.

GRAHAM DEAD BEAT ESCAPEMENT: invented by George Graham, increases accuracy in clocks.

GRANDE SONERIE: a full or grand strike. A clock or watch that strikes the hours and the quarters at each quarter.

JEWEL: semi-precious or synthetic stones used as bearings.

LANTERN CLOCK: the first domestic clock. A metal cased clock of the 14th to 17th centuries, originally made to hang on the wall and to be weight driven. Cases were made of iron, later of brass. Also known as Cromwellian, bedpost or bird cage clocks.

LION'S MASK: a decorative accessory formed of a lion's head with or without a ring passing through its mouth.

LONG CASE CLOCK: the horological term for a grandfather clock.

MAINSPRING: in a spring driven clock the mainspring supplies power.

MERCURY PENDULUM: invented by George Graham, 1721. The bob of a mercury pendulum consists of a container holding a quantity of mercury which compensates the elongation of the pendulum rod due to changes in temperature.

MORBIER CLOCK: known as Comtoise Clocks also. Morbier, France, the village where the clocks were produced, was in the Franche-Comte district. Made from the mid 1700's to 1900. Often marked with the name and address of the vendor, rarely with the name Morbier. Usually long case or lantern type. Fitted originally with a long pendulum verge escapement, later with anchor escapement. Characteristic is the straight or upright rack to the striking mechanism.

MOVEMENT: the "works" of a clock.

OGEE, O.G.: a term applied to cases of certain American clocks, because the front moulding is shaped in a ogee curve, one side convex the other concave.

ORIGINAL GLASS/TABLET: the painted glass panel on the door or front of many old clocks.

ORMULU: gilt made from finely ground gold and mercury.

PENDULUM: used to regulate clock movement, swings back and forth under the combined forces of gravity and momentum.

PLATES: the front and back of the clock movement.

POSTMAN'S ALARM: a 30-hour hanging clock; weight driven, long pendulum, circular dial. Case made of wood, fitted with alarm mechanism. Usually of Dutch origin.

PLINTH: the base.

PORCELAIN DIAL: a dial made with porcelain enamel.

SUSPENSION: means by which the suspension is hung.

SPELTER: lead alloy.

SWEEP SECONDS HAND: centrally mounted hand that sweeps the full area of the dial.

TIC-TAC: French drum clock with a recoil escapement and bob pendulum. Clocks of this type can be moved without removing the pendulum.

TING-TANG: sounds on two gongs or bells, usually one of a lower tone in ding-dong fashion at the quarters and at the hours. At the hour eight blows are struck followed by the number of hours. Two blows indicate first quarter, four the half hour and six quarter to the hour.

TRAIN: wheels and pinions of a clock.

VERGE: the pallet axis of a clock.

WESTMINSTER CHIME: the chime of Westminster bells.

BIBLIOGRAPHY

DESJARDINS, Rene   Clocks With Personalite. The Author. Hollywood. 1976.

DREPPARD, Carl W.   American Clocks & Clockmakers. Doubleday & Company Inc. New York. 1947.

MILLER, Robert W.   Clock Guide Identification With Prices. Wallace-Homestead Co. Des Moines. 1971.

PALMER, Brooks   A Treasury of American Clocks. The Macmillan Company. New York. 1966.

TYLER, E.J.   European Clocks. Ward Lock & Company Limited. London & Sydney. 1968.

ULLYETT, Kenneth   In Quest of Clocks. Rockliff Publishing Corporation Ltd. London. 1950.

UNITT, Doris & Peter   Arthur Pequegnat Clocks: With History & Price Guide. Clock House Publications. Peterborough. 1987.

Unitt's Price Guide to Clocks in Canada. Clock House Publications. Peterborough. 1981.

VARKARIS, Jane & Costas   The Pequegnat Story. Kendall/Hunt Publishing Company. Dubuque. 1982.

VARKARIS, Jane and James E. Connel   The Canada and Hamilton Clock Companies. The Boston Mills Press. Erin. 1986.

INDEX

125

CLOCK HOUSE COLLECTOR BOOKS

"UNITT'S CANADIAN PRICE GUIDE TO ANTIQUES & COLLECTABLES"
BOOK 10 (1984) $14.95, BOOK 13 (1990) $15.95, BOOK 14 (1991) $15.95
The guide with prices and photographs gathered from the Canadian market-
place......each guide is illustrated throughout with new photographs of antiques
and collectables for sale at antique stores, shows, sales, etc.

"UNITT'S BOOK OF MARKS ON ANTIQUES & COLLECTABLES" $14.95
Revised and Expanded
Contains maker's marks on antiques, such as Canadian silversmiths' marks;
British Hall marks; Silverplate marks of Canadian manufacturers; marks on art
glass; cut glass; bottles, etc; ceramics; china; pottery and porcelain.

"UNITT'S BOTTLES & VALUES & MORE" $15.95
Articles and information about methods of bottle making and Canadian
manufacturers. Hundreds of bottles illustrated and priced.

"UNITT'S CANADIAN PRICE GUIDE TO DOLLS & TOYS" Revised $16.95
This guide shows Canadian dolls, their makers and marks; European and
American dolls are included. Doll furniture and accessories are illustrated. Various
types of toys are shown and priced.

"PETER's CLOCK BOOK" $7.95
Illustrated step-by-step guide to cleaning spring-or weight-driven clocks......plus
hints on restoring cases.

"CANADIAN HANDBOOK OF PRESSED GLASS TABLEWARE" $24.95
An essential reference book. Direct and concise information on Canadian pressed
glass with 600 black and white photographs of over 230 patterns. Factories,
alternate names, and forms known are listed with each pattern.

"AMERICAN & CANADIAN GOBLETS" Volume I $19.95
Over 1,000 Canadian and American goblets are illustrated, cross-referenced, and
indexed in this well received book. A most comprehensive work on the subject
having many examples not previously shown.

CATALOGUE REPRINTS — Primary source material such as reprints of
Canadian manufacturers' catalogues are a valuable research aid to collectors.

"TORONTO SILVERPLATE CO., 1888 CATALOGUE" $10.95
......illustrates and gives original prices for plated articles manufactured by this
firm.

More Fitzhenry & Whiteside titles:

"HOW TO RESTORE AND REPAIR PRACTICALLY EVERYTHING"
Revised Edition by Lorraine Johnson $19.95
Superly illustrated guide to restoration; an indispensable source information
ranging from restoring stained-glass panels to rethreading pearls.

"THE MONTHLY EPIC — A History of Canadian Magazines" by Fraser
Sutherland $40.00
Meticulously researched, fact-filled yet accessible, illustrated history of magazine
publishing and the social developments of 200 years.

"RESTORING CANADIAN HOMES — A Sourcebook of Supplies and
Services" by John Hearn $23.95
Thoroughly illustrated with photos and line drawings. Stories of restorations and
the many people and sources of materials.

For a current list of our books for collectors, write to:
Fitzhenry & Whiteside
195 Allstate Pkwy.
Markham, Ont. L3R 4T8